ZENSHO W. KOPP

The light of wisdom

In inner silence, in the stillness of the heart, the light of the wisdom of all Buddhas shines forth.

This perfect, all-pervading Buddha-mind is without obstacles, immeasurable, vast and boundless. Free of all existential form, it is omnipresent in the entire universe. It is timeless eternity and is aware of itself as brightly shining light, brighter than a thousand suns.

Immerse yourself in your innermost being and return to this divine source of your true being.

When you experience your true self as being completely one with the self of all beings, you hold the pure seal of the Buddha Dharma in your hand.

In the midst of the spiritual delusion of this world, you live in vivacious awareness and beyond all differentiation in the enlightening wisdom of non-duality. You live in harmony with heaven and earth and pass through birth and death as if through an open gate.

Devotion to the Eternal is when you become inwardly empty, open and transparent to transcendence. When all of a sudden the constant flow of thinking ceases, your original, true being is revealed to you brightly and clearly.

Our discriminating, conceptual thinking must therefore remain silent if we wish to hear the divine Word that speaks itself in the innermost depths of our heart.

This silence in the face of the infinite is an inner process of emptying oneself and then becoming imbued with the all-pervading fullness of divine presence.

When you hear the news of someone's death, you should always realise that your life is also fleeting and you will die with absolute certainty. Only the time of your death is uncertain.

This inescapable certainty should inspire you to stop wasting your time with worldly trivialities and to make even greater efforts on the spiritual path. So live your life in such a way that you can die in the next moment without regret.

Turn your consciousness inwards and do not deviate from the clear self-awareness of your mind – your immortal, true essential nature.

This essential realisation of unity with the divine One Mind will become your protective shell at the moment of death.

But without having prepared yourself for death in this way during your life and wanting to make up for it quickly at the moment of death is like quickly digging a well when your house is already burning and on fire.

When we are out in nature, it is completely unnecessary to define the birds, flowers and trees with our autonomous urge of conceptual labelling.

This habit of limiting nature to a conceptual fixation alienates us from the living experience because true, pure feeling has already been replaced by a dead concept and robbed of its vitality.

Thus, through this concept of distorted dualistic perception, we miss out on the beauty and real experience of being that only reveals itself to our direct, pure perception.

When we have special experiences that touch our innermost being, which are in complete contrast to our general, intellectually limited ideas, we become inwardly still. We take a step back and begin to reflect on the meaning and meaninglessness of our externalised life.

This is the blessed moment in which our true, divine self shines through and calls on us to go beyond the limited mind.

What prevents true knowledge and spiritual realisation is the fact that people cannot recognise what reality is because of their pre-existing, preconceived ideas and can thus only see their limited conception of reality.

However, all intellectual theories are limited and wrong. The mind cannot be free of preconceived ideas because it is itself a manifestation of concepts.

Higher realisation will therefore only happen when we free ourselves from the concepts that prevent us from seeing clearly.

The pseudo-self, the ego delusion, has no real existence. It is nothing more than an energetic movement in which the ego attaches itself to everything in the manner of grasping and rejecting through the certainty of its own mortality.

Without this process of identification, the ego-consciousness could not maintain its delusion of its individual uniqueness, which is always in danger of dissolving.

In recognising and realising the non-duality of all being, we enter into the realm of the boundless freedom of the Zen mind. It is a realisation of clear consciousness and the experience of being completely at one with everything.

Thus, when we are clearly conscious in the present moment, then sweeping a staircase is just as sacred as lighting incense in a temple.

Zen is the truth beyond words and does not offer any erudite, philosophical explanations. With immediate directness, it always refers to the matter itself in order to remove the ground from under all theoretical cleverness.

Zen says: "If you want to know what tea tastes like, drink tea."

Only when you immerse yourself in the ocean of wisdom of the brightly shining One Mind will you know what the truth is.

The radiant light of the divine omnipresence of the original, immeasurable One Mind, filled with wonders, permeates the entire universe.

In the very centre of your heart, it reveals itself as your true being – the eternal I Am.

Awaken from the sleep of unconsciousness to this, your true being and you realise that nothing exists separately and outside the self, for everything is the One Mind, beside which nothing else exists.

In this external world of phenomena, everything is subject to change and thus birth and death. Yet the true self does not die. It is ageless and unchanging and therefore cannot be affected by death.

For this reason, at the moment of your death, you should surrender yourself completely to what is taking place, full of trust and devotion. The moment when all your clinging to the delusion of an ego collapses, the radiant light of the One Mind appears and will receive you.

When you spend your life in mindless routine and indifferent unconsciousness, you miss out on the constant presence of divine being, which reveals itself Here-Now in all its fullness.

Divine reality is absolute Now and can therefore only be experienced in the conscious presence of clear spiritual alertness in Here and Now.

Recognising ourselves means recognising God, for our true self is divine reality. In its omnipresence, it permeates the entire universe and shines forth from all things.

True self-realisation therefore means nothing other than becoming completely one with the all-encompassing wholeness of all being.

It is a returning to our original state beyond birth and death.

If you look up at the cloudy sky in the evening and do not see the moon, you might say: "There's no moon today."

But the moon is always there, just like the self-radiating Self-Mind that shines from behind the dark clouds of discriminating, conceptual thinking.

The One Mind is always present, only you are not present.

Every awakened person who has the desire to communicate his experience of highest reality beyond birth and death to other people must learn that very few are interested.

What he has to say to others is like the light of the blinding midday sun to them, so that they prefer to retreat into the more comfortable semi-darkness of mindless routine and indifferent spiritual unconsciousness.

Why bother with the rubbish of intellectual speculation, brought on through philosophical erudition? What use could there be in rummaging around like a goat in every corner and taking a load of old rubbish into your mouth?

Instead, reach into your own treasure, for the truth you seek is closer than you can imagine – it is within you.

The radiant clarity of the One Mind is omnipresent, all-pervading and is absolute reality.

Its true nature in its purity is like the marvellous sparkling radiance of a flawless crystal ball and is never clouded by the befoulment of samsara.

This mind – our true self – is Buddha from the beginning on.

The question: "Where are we after death?" is a misguided, completely wrong question. Instead, the correct question is: "What are we after death?"

A deceased person, that is, their essential consciousness, does not reach this other state of being, this other dimension, by travelling in the sense of movement in space and time.

Instead, they reach it through a transition in consciousness.

When you truly love, you experience that true love always happens when you do not just see the other person but that you recognise them as belonging to yourself. You experience such a great connection and unity with them that you experience them as part of yourself.

This real, true love is always ready to give of itself without asking for anything.

True love demands nothing at all, it only strives for unity.

The radiant light of your true self shines at the very centre of your heart but you do not see it.

Turn inwards, go into yourself, immerse yourself in the space deep inside your heart and in one blessed moment, the wisdom eye of realisation will open to you.

The shackles of your attachment to birth and death fall away from you and you stand in the cloudless, radiant glory of your true being.

The Buddha's smile is filled with quiet serenity and inner peace since it expresses boundless love, all-encompassing compassion and benevolence.

Every truly enlightened person lives in the awake presence of clear awareness of the present moment and thus radiates inner peace in a very natural way. It is a peace that radiates outwards and transforms those who are ready to receive it.

Those who have awakened to the reality of their true self live in harmony with heaven and earth in the all-encompassing wholeness of being. This is reflected in their open heart and their compassionate love for all beings.

They fight and argue with no one, for they have conquered themselves.

In order to become spiritually free and to have a creative consciousness it is necessary that we go beyond the limited patterns of discriminating thinking and our clinging to the memory of our dead past.

This is because clinging to our past identity only reinforces the ego concept and prevents any true spiritual transformation.

The realisation of equanimity is one of the essential elements of Buddhism. Yet equanimity is all too easily misunderstood as indifference. Indifference only reinforces the ego delusion because it is the result of mental inertia and lack of compassion for the suffering of other beings.

True equanimity, on the other hand, means maintaining an all-encompassing love and steadfastness of the mind in all situations of daily life.

We are the result of a conditioned, limited worldview, based on our thinking and our ignorance of the true self.

The path to realising our true, original being therefore begins with recognising the unchanging mind-essence within us. This is the pure light of the mind and can only be experienced in the innermost depths of the heart, in a state of perfect stillness of mind.

It is your true essence, the brightly gleaming reality of your true being, which dissolves all illusions.

"The thunderclap in a clear, blue sky" in the language of Zen is the enlightenment experience of suddenly awakening from the dream of body, mind and world. However, this will only happen with absolute certainty when you are free from the fear of not returning to life after mystical death.

It only happens when you least expect it and the illusory ego has completely surrendered.

In detaching ourselves from our dualistic, limited view of me and you, of subject and object, we achieve a serene, spontaneous connection with all beings, imbued with natural friendliness.

This liberation from our egocentric mindset leads us to be free and in perfect harmony with all phenomena.

The question of birth and death – as far as the true self is concerned – is complete nonsense.

Nobody comes and goes. You are infinite, beyond the illusion of space and time because your true being is timeless eternity. There is no individual, single self, so what could come and go?

Become aware, awaken to the reality of your true self, and the dream of body, mind and world and coming and going dissolves.

It is the divine One Mind itself that moves us to seek God and become one with Him. So we seek Him in holy places such as churches, temples and distant lands.

But at some point, after a long search, we finally find our way back to ourselves and realise that He, whom we were looking for on the outside, was always present as our true being in our innermost being.

The ego is nothing more than an unconscious reaction mechanism. It is not a conscious intelligence and therefore its reactions to certain circumstances are usually very uncontrolled.

Often they even contradict our common sense and can be extremely childish.

The ego can only be controlled through the absolute presence of spiritual awareness and inner calm and serenity.

We are like the waves on the surface of the ocean. As individual waves, we are constantly dying and being reborn, over and over again. The only unchanging thing beyond all change is the ocean.

However, the wave is the ocean and thus are we the One Mind. Our true being is unchanging and beyond birth and death. This means that we are immortal.

To awaken to your immortal, true self, you do not actually need to do anything at all since it is your inherent, true nature and not a matter of attainment.

So sit down, remain detached and relaxed and stay in awareness of mind. However, since you are constantly under the inner urge to do something, you will have many thoughts running through your head.

Yet no matter what happens, remain clearly aware in your natural state, just observe – be an uninvolved witness without reference, and meditation takes place all of its own accord.

Zen is the truth beyond all words and rises above the narrow limits of discriminating, conceptual thinking. Its profound truth is beyond what can be explained intellectually and can only be understood through direct, intuitive insight.

This is why Zen is the most secret, direct and highest path to liberation – to Buddhahood.

It has only one goal: the knowledge and realisation of the true nature of the mind, our true being beyond birth and death.

Only when you have reached the limits of your spiritual struggle will the truth you seek reveal itself to you. When all concepts of your discriminating, conceptual thinking are exhausted, the bright, original light appears above you and you rise above space and time and all illusions.

The dream of body, mind and world dissolves into the radiant glory of the One Mind – your original, true being.

At the moment of your awakening from the dream of body, mind and world, the boundless expanse of your true being is revealed that instant. The whole illusory world of appearances dissolves into the marvellous sparkling radiance of transcendent reality.

The wall of death is broken through, the veil of maya is torn apart and the radiant light of your true self shines forth.

In the certainty of the emptiness of all that exists, gained through meditative clear vision of mind, we recognise that all things are the illusionary, magical expression of our own mind.

This means that the outer world of appearances is in its true essence the same as the mind that perceives it.

The non-existent appears real and clear like the reflection of the moon in water.

Our ego-induced separation from the all-encompassing wholeness of being is an alienation from life, which becomes unfulfilled and problematic as a result.

As a consequence of our separate existence, we feel cut off from other beings. We are insecure and confused and transfer our desire for security to external objects and people.

Yet it is only when we see through the illusory nature and emptiness of all phenomena that the realisation of the inseparable unity of all life is revealed.

Spiritual realisation presupposes the profound insight into your non-separateness from all beings.

Such a holistic openness includes an all-encompassing empathy with the suffering beings, trapped in the cycle of existence. For wherever your consciousness is unable to reach with all its senses and powers, it can reach through the power of divine love.

This requires a fundamental spiritual attitude that is open to life in its universality, without any limitations.

The master's words are the finger that points to the moon. The moon is reality, the finger is only the hint.

However, you confuse the finger with what it points to. You study the finger. You study the various philosophies and religions and believe you will find the truth that way.

Yet the moon is the truth you are looking for, not the finger.

Nothing is really more important in life than realising our true being.

But in reality, no external effort is required and we do not need to go anywhere to recognise our true, immortal nature.

The wave on the surface of the ocean does not need to look for the ocean anywhere because it is the ocean itself.

We are what we are looking for. What we want to become, we already are at the very core of our being, we just have to recognise it.

The true self is the One Mind, beside which nothing else exists; it is the sole Being, like the ocean and its waves and must therefore be seen and experienced as an all-encompassing whole.

So allow your mind to be vast and open like boundless space and free yourself from your dualistic, discriminating way in which you view things.

In the mirror-clear awareness of the mind, you penetrate directly into the true essence of all things.

True Zen consciousness permeates everything each moment with a clear mind, is inwardly detached from external phenomena and acts freely and un- bound everywhere in perfect harmony.

Habituate your mind in letting it dwell in the ab- solute presence of the immediate present in silent self-awareness in everything you do and wherever you are.

Only when you experience stillness as life can you perceive your divine being.

Love, which is God Himself, is pure, spiritual awareness and all-encompassing, multidimensional consciousness that recognises and loves itself in everything.

When your heart is filled with divine love, there is nothing that you see as separate from you because true love does not see separating multiplicity, but instead recognises in everything a revelation of the One in its boundless diversity.

In truth, there is no self that is bound to the cycle of birth and death. The idea of a personal ego is the actual bondage.

Real, true individuality is only realised when we free ourselves from the unyielding shackles of our concepts. Then we rise above the dark mists of appearances into the radiant light of our true being and realise our Buddha nature.

True renunciation is not a denial of the world or an escape into loneliness, but rather that you renounce the ego, your ego conception, together with the interwoven memories of your dead past.

True renunciation does not mean that you renounce external things and feel contempt towards the world but rather, it is when you detach yourself from your ego delusion with its belief in individual uniqueness and its inner attachment to things.

Our true, divine self is pure identity, the eternal "I am". It is Being in itself, which is aware of itself, and therefore absolute consciousness. This means that God is consciousness and should be revered as pure, absolute consciousness.

The general idea of a God of unattainable transcendence is blasphemy and blatant materialism. If small children believe in a God in heaven, that is fine, but if grown-ups cling to this infantile notion, it is a fatal error.

The peaceful, self-contained, clear mind is our reality. When thoughts arise, it becomes restless, but when the thoughts fade, it calms down and becomes still and clear.

Modest simplicity of mind leads to stillness. In this stillness – the silence in the face of the infinite – the true self reveals itself.

Only when we free ourselves from our inner restlessness with the compulsive desire to strive away from Now and the constant urge to have to do something, do we approach the peace and freedom of the kingdom of God within us.

Meditation without true devotion to the highest reality of the One Mind is without heart. For only through sincere devotion will your meditation attain real depth and clarity.

Only through this unshakeable trust in your true, immortal self, which you always carry in your inner-most being, can you awaken to your true nature.

Then you will come face to face with the original Buddha of your own mind.

To realise the truth of Zen, it is necessary to complement clear thinking with intuition and to balance sitting in contemplation with active action.

Shatter the knot of duality and you realise the wisdom of non-duality.

The true path of Zen is beyond all distinction between sacred and profane. It is the everyday mind that is completely free from all acceptance and rejection.

In the realisation of this nondiscriminating mental clarity, you attain steadfastness of mind in every situation in life.

The whole external world of appearance that you experience has no real, substantial being in itself. It has no more reality than the dream you dreamt last night.

Nothing is outside your inherent consciousness.

When you attain non-discerning clarity, the mind and the outer world of appearances are one.

The universal law of eternal transformation of all being is the great transformation that ultimately dissolves everything into ultimate reality.

Therefore, hold on to nothing, be as vast and open as the sky and you will be in perfect harmony with the universal law of transformation.

In this spiritual realisation, you experience the immutable in the midst of all change.

Imprint

First edition 2024
Original title "**Das Licht der Weisheit**"
published by Spirit Rainbow Verlag, Aachen, Germany 2024

Original idea and design: Verena Kopp
Image editing: Reinhard Zanella
Translation: John Kitching
Typesetting/ Cover design: Reinhard Zanella
Project coordination: Jörg Zimmermann
Back cover photo: Axel Jung

Publisher: BoD · Books on Demand GmbH,
In de Tarpen 42, 22848 Norderstedt, bod@bod.de
Printed by: Libri Plureos GmbH, Friedensallee 273, 22763 Hamburg
© 2025 Zen Master Zensho W. Kopp
ISBN: 978-3-7597-7489-7

Zensho W. Kopp, born 1938, is one of the most significant spiritual masters of our present times and teaches a contemporary path to spiritual realisation. The internationally renowned author of numerous Zen books and audio books instructs a large community of students and directs the Zen Center Tao Chan in Wiesbaden, Germany.

Tao Chan Zentrum e.V., Non-profit society, Wiesbaden.
More info at: **www.tao-chan.org**

Twice a month, the Zen Center Tao Chan organises a Zen-evening with a talk by Zen Master Zensho W. Kopp, where guests are welcome to attend. There is also the possibility for asking Zen Master Zensho questions.

Register here for the evening:
www.tao-chan.org/events/events-zen-night.html

Subscribe here for free short talks by Zen Master Zensho W. Kopp:
www.youtube.com/@zencentertaochan/shorts
www.youtube.com/@zencentertaochan

Facebook site for the Zen Center Tao Chan
www.facebook.com/zencentertaochan

Image credits